20TH CENTURY MUSIC
1970s
YEARS OF EXCESS

20TH CENTURY MUSIC – 1970s
was produced by

David West  Children's Books
7 Princeton Court
55 Felsham Road
London SW15 1AZ

Picture Research: Carrie Haines
Designer: Rob Shone
Editor: James Pickering

First published in Great Britain in 2001 by
Heinemann Library, Halley Court, Jordan Hill,
Oxford OX2 8EJ, a division of Reed Educational and
Professional Publishing Limited.

OXFORD MELBOURNE AUCKLAND
JOHANNESBURG BLANTYRE GABORONE
IBADAN PORTSMOUTH (NH) USA CHICAGO

05 04 03 02 01
10 9 8 7 6 5 4 3 2 1

ISBN 0 431 14214 9 (HB)
ISBN 0 431 14221 1 (PB)

British Library Cataloguing in Publication Data

Hayes, Malcolm
The 70s: years of excess. - (20th century music)
1. Music - 20th century - Juvenile literature
I. Title II. Nineteen seventies
780.9'04

Printed and bound in Italy

PHOTO CREDITS :
Abbreviations: t-top, m-middle, b-bottom, r-right,
l-left.

Front cover m - (Ian Dickson) Redferns, br - Jonathan
Smith/Lebrecht Collection. 4m & 12bl, 6b, 11tl, 12m
& b, 12-13t, 13tr, 26ml, 27mr - Betty
Freeman/Lebrecht collection. 9t, 10m, 26tr - David
Farrell/Lebrecht Collection. 28 both, 29tr - Nigel
Luckhurst/Lebrecht Collection. 9b, 11tr - George
Newson/Lebrecht Collection. 7t - Suzie
Maeder/Lebrecht Collection. 8t - S.
Lauterwasser/Lebrecht Collection. 8b -
IRCAM/Lebrecht Collection. 9m - Horst
Tappe/Lebrecht Collection. 27tl - Richard H.
Smith/Lebrecht Collection. 27b - Mike Evans/Lebrecht
Collection. 29l - Jonathan Smith/Lebrecht Collection.
11br - Lebrecht Collection. 5b & 23b, 18mr, 20ml &
tr, 21mr (Michael Ochs Archive), 3, 14t, 19ml &br,
21b, 24b, 25 all (David Redfern), 19tr, 22t, 23tl & mr
(Richie Aaron), 14b, 15t & b (Fin Costello), 17br,
22b, 24l (Gems), 4b (Crixpix), 13b (Mick Gold), 15m
(Mick Hutson), 16t (Dave Ellis), 16m (Max Redfern),
16b (Glenn A. Baker Archive), 17l (Debi Doss), 18bl
(A. Putler), 21tl (RB) - Redferns. 6t, 7m & b, 10b -
Hulton Getty. 4t - The Kobal Collection. 5t - Rex
Features.

Front cover: Led Zeppelin (main image), Dmitri
Shostakovich.

The dates in brackets after a person's name
give the years that he or she lived.

An explanation of difficult words can be
found in the glossary on page 30.

20TH CENTURY MUSIC

1970s

YEARS OF EXCESS

Malcolm Hayes

Heinemann
LIBRARY

CONTENTS

NEW YORK'S VERY OWN
Barbra Streisand (born 1942) developed parallel and often overlapping careers in film and music, sometimes writing her own songs. Her albums included The Owl and the Pussycat *(1971),* Classical Barbra *(1976, featuring songs by Debussy and Schumann) and* A Star is Born *(1976).*

MINIMALIST FORCE
Besides his appearances with the Philip Glass Ensemble (below), Glass (born 1937) also composed minimalist operas.

CAROLE KING
Born Carole Klein in 1942, the Brooklyn singer's status as the best-selling female songwriter to date was confirmed by her albums Tapestry *(1971),* Music *(1972) and* Thoroughbred *(1976).*

THE END OF INNOCENCE

ROCK OPERA
The Who's Pete Townshend (left) created Tommy *and its most famous song, 'Pinball Wizard', performed here by the group in Ken Russell's 1975 film, with Keith Moon (drums) and John Entwistle (bass guitar).*

In the Sixties, revolution had been (mostly) fun. In the Seventies, revolution became nasty.

Many European states had to cope with politically motivated terrorism by radical extremists. Economic and political instability brought rampant inflation, and with it public and trade union unrest. And in 1975, the United States had to come to terms with defeat and withdrawal from its war in South Vietnam against the Communist-led North. Music reflected this decade of turbulence and disillusion. Rock developed into a culture of deliberate excess. Concerts became gigantically amplified, semi-theatrical mass events that filled huge stadiums. Then classical music began to react against this. The rise of minimalism, at first mainly on America's west coast, placed a new emphasis on a musical style that was seen to be 'cool'. Eventually there was a political reaction too. Margaret Thatcher's election as Britain's Prime Minister in 1979 began a new era of Conservative government, which was soon followed by the start of Ronald Reagan's presidency in the US. For the time being, the revolution was over.

JAMAICAN MINSTREL
Bob Marley (1945–81) helped to make reggae a major musical force for black people.

ITALY AND GERMANY: THE POLITICAL LEFT

Politically, the waves in many European countries rolled very high. For a time it seemed possible that Portugal and Italy, for instance, might become Communist states. There was equally fierce resistance from the centre and the right. Composers, too, became involved.

MUSIC FOR THE REVOLUTION

Luigi Nono (1924–90) at first continued his personal left-wing musical crusade. *Como una Ola de Fuerza y Luz* (Like a Wave of Fire and Light, 1972) for soprano, piano, orchestra and electronic tape is a homage to a hero of the Chilean left. From the mid-Seventies, however, the tone of Nono's music began to change. *Sofferte Onde Serene* (Serene Waves Suffered, 1976), for piano and tape, and *Con Luigi Dallapiccola* (With Luigi Dallapiccola, 1979), for six percussionists and live electronics, are both non-political works written in memory of friends; Dallapiccola (1904–75) was one of Italy's major 20th-century composers.

BRANCHING OUT
Nono's political works of the early Seventies often used unconventional mixed media. Y Entonces Comprendió (And Then He Understood, 1970), the composer's homage to the Cuban revolution, was scored for six female voices and electronic tape. The musical result was both confrontational and colourful.

MUSICAL NON-CONFORMIST
America's Frederic Rzewski (born 1938) is a classical composer-pianist who has worked also with jazz musicians. Rzewski's left-wing political stance is apparent in *Coming Together* (1972), which sets the words of an inmate at the 1971 uprising in New York's Attica Prison. *Winsboro Cotton Mill Blues* (1979) for piano is based on a 1930s song about working in a mill in North Carolina.

Since the mid-Sixties, Rzewski has worked frequently in Europe.

6

HENZE GOES TO CUBA

Germany's Hans Werner Henze (born 1926) was also committed to a left-wing stance which was deepened by his first visit to the Communist state of Cuba in 1969–70. *El Cimarrón* (1970), for baritone singer and three players, tells the story of a Cuban runaway slave in the 19th century. Henze also continued to write for western symphony orchestras. *Heliogabalus Imperator* (1972) is a sumptuously written symphonic poem about a corrupt emperor of Ancient Rome.

EXOTIC REVOLUTION
Henze's music of the Seventies blended strident confrontation with alluring sound. His experiences in Cuba added the sounds of Latin American percussion to his music.

SEDUCTIVE SOUNDS
Luciano Berio skilfully balanced the aggressive stance of his music with its need to sound attractive to audiences.

RADICAL POLITICS, RADICAL ATTITUDE

Luciano Berio (born 1925) preferred a slightly less strident left-wing stance. His stage work *Opera* (1970) explored what Berio saw as the decline of opera itself and the middle class society that created it, while *Coro* (Chorus, 1976) for chorus and orchestra sets a broad range of left-wing and folk texts.

POLITICAL BARRIER
Isolating West Berlin within Communist East Germany, the Berlin Wall symbolized a deeply divided European continent. Almost everyone who tried to escape over it to the West was shot by East German border guards.

EXOTIC WORLDS: EUROPE AND THE EAST

The heroes of the former avant-garde had now each developed an agenda of their own. Some expanded and refined their existing personal style. Others searched insistently for new sounds, and new ways of creating them.

MUSICAL PROPHET

Pierre Boulez's firm belief in the radical possibilities of music's future was given a new outlet by the foundation of IRCAM, which was created for him with the personal support of France's President Pompidou.

SOUNDS OF THE FUTURE

Pierre Boulez (born 1925) and Karlheinz Stockhausen (born 1928) had once been close colleagues, but they were now following different musical paths. Boulez worked mostly at IRCAM (Institut de Recherche et Coordination Acoustique/Musique), a centre in Paris created for him and other composers to explore the possibilities of computer-generated musical sound. Stockhausen's *Trans* (1971), for instruments and electronic tape, and *Inori* (1974) for orchestra were semi-theatrical works that overlapped with rock.

THE IRCAM CENTRE

Ever since the electronic experiments of the Fifties, composers had been aware that the possibilities of transforming traditional musical sounds, or of generating entirely new ones, were almost unlimited. IRCAM's intended purpose was to channel these possibilities in a creative direction. This blueprint shows a layout of IRCAM and its equipment.

le bâtiment et ses équipements

MESSIAEN'S CANYONS

Olivier Messiaen (1908–92) continued to create works glorifying both the Catholic faith, and what was for him its purest image in nature: the sounds of birdsong. *Des Canyons aux Etoiles* (From the Canyons to the Stars, 1974) was a huge, 12-movement work for solo piano, horn and orchestra. It was inspired by Messiaen's visit to Bryce Canyon in the American state of Utah.

A VOICE FROM JAPAN

Toru Takemitsu (1930–96) had become the leading voice among Japanese composers. His music beautifully expressed an oriental spirit through western musical media, as in his orchestral work *A Flock Descends into the Pentagonal Garden* (1977). György Ligeti (born 1923) further extended his adventurous experiments in theatre and sound, and combined these in his witty and outrageous opera *Le Grand Macabre* (1978). His major instrumental works included *Clocks and Clouds* (1973) for chorus and orchestra.

Menuhin with violin and Shankar with sitar

SHANKAR AND MENUHIN

Ravi Shankar (born 1920) has made it his life's mission to bring Indian classical music to the peoples of the West. In the same spirit, he has also collaborated with western musicians. Shankar found a kindred spirit in the celebrated violinist Yehudi Menuhin (1916–99), who was himself deeply interested in Indian culture, history, tradition and thought.

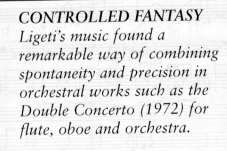

CONTROLLED FANTASY

Ligeti's music found a remarkable way of combining spontaneity and precision in orchestral works such as the Double Concerto (1972) for flute, oboe and orchestra.

EASTERN VISITOR

Takemitsu's interest in creating straightforwardly beautiful sounds made him and his music a welcome presence at western musical events. He is pictured here during a visit to the Aldeburgh Festival in Suffolk.

AMERICAN INDIVIDUALISTS

True to form, the finest of America's senior composers refused to conform to surrounding trends, persisting instead with their different operations, however unfashionable. And in Mexico City, Conlon Nancarrow, one of the most gifted, suddenly resurfaced after years of obscurity and neglect.

BERNSTEIN KEEPS EXPLORING

Leonard Bernstein (1918–90) was as busy as ever as a world-famous conductor. He also composed a ballet, *Dybbuk* (1974), and an orchestral song-cycle, *Songfest* (1977). His semi-theatre work *Mass* (1971) was a mixed success. So was *1600 Pennsylvania Avenue*, a musical with lyrics by Alan Jay Lerner. Composed for America's Bicentennial celebrations in 1976, this portrays a sequence of Presidents and First Ladies through the ages.

UNIQUE TALENT
Conlon Nancarrow (1912–97) settled in Mexico City in 1940. There he began to compose a brilliantly inventive sequence of Studies for player-piano, composing the music by punching the holes in the instrument's paper rolls. This made possible fantastically complex rhythms, although some of the simpler Studies have since been arranged for piano or chamber orchestra.

CROSSING OVER
Some of Bernstein's greatest successes as a conductor were with European orchestras, notably the Vienna Philharmonic.

THE USA'S 200TH BIRTHDAY
The 1976 anniversary of the Declaration of Independence was marked by important commissions for American composers, including Bernstein and Carter.

Nancarrow had studied classical music, and played trumpet in a jazz band. Both of these influences shaped the rhythmic strength of his music.

REAPING THE HARVEST

Besides his renewed interest in composing vocal works, Carter completed his Third String Quartet in 1971, and a Duo for violin and piano in 1974.

CARTER: SYMPHONIES AND SONG-CYCLES

Elliott Carter (born 1908) was now an established elder statesman of modernism. His typically complex and dramatic Symphony of Three Orchestras (1976) was commissioned for the Bicentennial. Carter then composed two song-cycles on texts by American poets: *A Mirror on which to Dwell* (1975, words by Elizabeth Bishop) and *Syringa* (1978, words by John Ashbery).

INSPIRATION

Crumb has said that his music draws on the natural sounds and acoustic he 'inherited' from the hills surrounding his birthplace in Charleston, West Virginia.

MUSIC OF CHILDREN AND ANGELS

George Crumb (born 1929) suddenly became internationally famous with two dark and powerful chamber works. Each one draws together a remarkable range of sounds and musical styles. Crumb's song-cycle *Ancient Voices of Children* (1970) sets words by the Spanish poet Federico García Lorca, while *Black Angels* (1970) is for an electronically amplified string quartet whose members also play percussion instruments. Another atmospheric chamber work followed: *Vox Balaenae* (Voice of the Whale, 1971), based on the recorded 'singing' of humpback whales.

MINIMALISM

Minimalism has been around for centuries: composers as different as Beethoven, Wagner and Sibelius knew how to use repeated and overlapping melodic and rhythmic patterns as an effective musical device. Minimalist composers now went further, building entire works in this way.

PHILIP GLASS

Besides performing his instrumental works with his own ensemble, Philip Glass (born 1937) also composed for the theatre. *Einstein on the Beach* (1976) was a collaboration with the theatre director Robert Wilson, while *Satyagraha* (1979) portrayed Mahatma Gandhi's early life and his philosophy of non-violent political resistance. Glass's brand of minimalism is generally more driving and insistent than Reich's or Adams's.

Glass (lower right) in rehearsal

STEVE REICH
Minimalist music's 'easy listening' appeal disguises the reality that it can be extremely demanding to perform: navigating through the gradual phase-changes requires exceptionally secure nerves and concentration. Like Glass and others Reich tackled the problem by founding his own ensemble.

PHASES AND PATTERNS

Like Philip Glass, Steve Reich (born 1936) formed his own ensemble to play his music, including *Drumming* (1971), *Music for Mallet Instruments, Voices and Organ* (1973) and *Music for Eighteen Musicians* (1976). Influenced by African drumming and Balinese gamelan music, these works build large structures out of the simple principle of setting up overlapping musical patterns, and then shifting these gradually out of phase with each other to form new patterns. Terry Riley (born 1935) and La Monte Young (born 1935) explored similar musical territory in their own individual ways.

13

TERRY RILEY
Riley (left, seated) explored the possibilities of overlapping musical patterns on electronic keyboards. Both this and his interest in Indian music are apparent in The Persian Surgery Dervishes (1972).

LA MONTE YOUNG
During his studies with Stockhausen, Young (right) developed his minimalist concept of a drone-based music. This is performed with light shows devised by his wife, the artist Marian Zazeela.

A NEW NAME

John Adams (born 1947) first became interested in electronic music and then, influenced by Reich and others, began to develop a different style of composing. This combined minimalism's intricate pattern-making with the long-range harmonic reach of the classical symphonic tradition. *Shaker Loops* (1978) for instrumental ensemble marked Adams's arrival as a major talent.

TUBULAR BELLS SELLS (16 MILLION COPIES)

In 1973, 19-year-old Mike Oldfield (born 1953) recorded *Tubular Bells* for a new record label, set up for the project by an unknown mail-order record retailer called Richard Branson. Oldfield played most of the instruments himself in the studio version, and then conducted an orchestral arrangement in the concert hall. The huge success of this minimalist-rock album made Oldfield, Branson and Virgin Records world-famous.

MIKE OLDFIELD
While the classically trained Riley and Young found their music influencing rock, Oldfield made the process work in reverse. The orchestral arrangement of Tubular Bells was made by avant-garde classical composer David Bedford (born 1937).

HEAVY ROCK: LED ZEPPELIN

The explosive, electronically amplified sound of blues-rock had been developed in the Sixties by groups such as the Jimi Hendrix Experience and Cream. It continued to flourish in the Seventies, becoming even louder, heavier and more confrontational.

A BIT LOUDER THAN CLASSICAL

In 1973, after a tour of Japan, Deep Purple were officially credited in the *Guinness Book of Records* as the world's loudest band. Their style blended massively heavy rock with the classical interests of their keyboard player Jon Lord and guitarist Ritchie Blackmore. Their albums included *Deep Purple in Rock* (1970), *Machine Head* (1972) and the live double album *Made in Japan* (1973).

Plant (left) and Page of Led Zeppelin (pictured in their 1970s heyday) sometimes perform together today.

ROCK SUPREMACY

Led Zeppelin dominated Seventies rock almost as completely as the Beatles had reigned over the Sixties. In a sequence of legendary tours and albums – *Led Zeppelin III* (1970), the unnamed fourth album (1971) and *Physical Graffiti* (1975) – the band's style ranged from thunderously heavy blues to gentler folk, spurred on by Jimmy Page's ultra-powerful guitar-playing and Robert Plant's shrill-to-soft vocals.

EXECUTIVE TRANSPORT
Deep Purple travelled in a private Boeing 720 called Starship I. This was the age of excess, after all.

LIVE ACT
Performing with a live boa constrictor was a far-out idea even for the Seventies, but Alice Cooper did it. His snake was called Angela.

THE WILDER SHORES

The pounding, ear-blasting world of heavy metal was dominated by groups whose stage shows were as deliberately outrageous as the noise-level of their music. England's Black Sabbath were hugely successful on both sides of the Atlantic with their albums *Black Sabbath* and *Paranoid* (both 1970) and *Master of Reality* (1971). Even more notorious were the stage shows of America's Alice Cooper, named after the band's lead vocalist (whose real name was Vincent Furnier). Their albums *School's Out* (1972) and *Billion Dollar Babies* (1973) sold millions.

TAKING ON THE WORLD

Kiss were formed in New York in 1972, and quickly took America and then other territories by storm with their furiously loud and controversial live shows, which outraged large areas of conservative public opinion. They were even accused of flirting with Nazism (unlikely, given that some of the band's members were Jewish). Their most successful albums included *Hotter Than Hell* (1974), *Dressed to Kill* (1975) and *Destroyer* (1976).

NEW YORK HEROES
Bigger on American home ground than elsewhere, Kiss set out to challenge Led Zeppelin with their over-the-top stage show.

15

PROGRESSIVE ROCK: TULL AND YES

The Seventies was the heyday of massively amplified rock concerts in huge arenas, complete with light and laser shows. The appeal to audiences was often theatrical as much as musical.

Ian Anderson also plays guitar, sings and composes.

*SCI-FI ROCK
Yes's concerts were
magical events for their fans, who
flocked to hear the music of their albums
Tales from Topographic Oceans (1973)
and Relayer (1974)*

YES PROGRESS

Yes's performances and albums, including *Fragile (1971)* and *Close to the Edge* (1972), featured the virtuoso keyboard-playing of the classically trained Rick Wakeman. Emerson, Lake and Palmer had keyboard-player Keith Emerson, also classically trained. The group ambitiously fused rock and classical in *Tarkus* (1971) and *Pictures at an Exhibition* (also 1971), based on Mussorgsky's piano work (1874).

*ELP
Greg Lake (vocals and guitar, left), Carl Palmer (drums, centre) and Keith Emerson (keyboards, right) drew on musical resources ranging from Bartók to synthesizers.*

STAYING POWER

ethro Tull named themselves fter an 18th-century griculturalist. Their lead artist nd song-writer, Ian Anderson, pecialized in the classical lute, which he had learned fter first hearing jazz's multi-nstrumentalist, Roland Kirk. Huge album successes anged from *Aqualung* 1971) to *Thick as a Brick* (1972) and *Heavy Horses* (1978). The band still performs and records successfully today.

GENESIS TAKE OFF

Genesis was formed at England's Charterhouse public school. Key albums were *Foxtrot* (1972) and *Selling England by the Pound* (1973). World success continued after lead singer and songwriter Peter Gabriel left in 1975 and was replaced by the group's drummer-turned-singer Phil Collins. The Moody Blues continued their individual style of orchestral rock with *Seventh Sojourn* (1972). And Pink Floyd recorded one of the best-selling albums of all time in *Dark Side of the Moon* (1973).

BOWIE: THE ART OF SELF-INVENTION

David Bowie (born David Jones, 1947) swept to rock stardom by personifying the weird stage characters he invented for himself: Ziggy Stardust (as in *The Rise and Fall of Ziggy Stardust and the Spiders from Mars*, 1972) and Aladdin Sane (*Aladdin Sane*, 1973). In 1977, Bowie produced *The Idiot* and *Lust for Life*, recorded by the equally over-the-top Iggy Pop (born James Jewel Osterburg, 1947), and also collaborated with ex-Roxy Music keyboard-player Brian Eno (born 1948) in *Low* (1977). Bowie also produced the album *Transformer* (1972) by Lou Reed (born 1942).

MULTIPLE CHARACTERS
David Bowie's provocative gear-changes of image and musical personality encompassed his albums Diamond Dogs *(1974),* Station to Station *(1976) and* Heroes *(1977).*

DARK UNDERTONES
The allure of Lou Reed's songs in Berlin *(1973) and* Coney Island Baby *(1976) rubbed shoulders with an inner bleakness.*

JAZZ AND FUSION

Jazz, too, was experimenting with new ways of 'crossing over' with other kinds of music. Fusion in jazz was a cross-fertilization of the progressive jazz of the Sixties with elements of rock and, sometimes, also classical music.

THE MASTER RETIRES (FOR A WHILE)

Miles Davis (1926–91) explored further into jazz-rock fusion with *A Tribute to Jack Johnson* (1970) and other albums before a car crash and illness stopped him working for several years. Saxophonist Wayne Shorter (born 1933) founded Weather Report in 1970 with the Austrian-born keyboard player Joe Zawinul (born 1932) – both had earlier worked with Davis. Weather Report became one of the decade's major fusion bands.

18

ULTIMATE PIANIST

A child prodigy, Keith Jarrett (born 1945) developed from the start as a jazz pianist who also played classical. Besides collaborating with other musicians (among them Miles Davis and drummer Art Blakey), Jarrett has given solo concerts whose brilliance in improvization have gone into jazz legend, such as *The Köln Concert*, recorded live in 1975.

Keith Jarrett, admired by classical and jazz fans alike

'CHANGING FROM DAY TO DAY LIKE THE WEATHER'

This is how Joe Zawinul (keyboards, far left) described the music-making of the fusion band he co-founded with Wayne Shorter (tenor saxophone, second from left).

STAR PIANISTS

Chick Corea (born 1941) was already known as an exceptional piano and keyboard player, performing with Miles Davis among others. He now formed his own fusion band, Circle, and then left it in 1971 to set up another, Return to Forever, which played successfully throughout the Seventies. Oscar Peterson (born 1925) appeared mostly as a piano soloist from 1970 onwards, dazzling audiences on his popular television show with his vast technique.

JAZZ GOES EAST

Influenced by Indian philosophy and music, English guitarist John McLaughlin (born 1942) founded the five-strong Mahavishnu Orchestra in 1971 with drummer Billy Cobham (born 1944). Two of their finest albums were *The Inner Mounting Flame* (1971) and *Birds of Fire* (1972). McLaughlin also teamed up with the Californian rock group Santana in 1973. Two years later Cobham formed a new group, Spectrum. Freddie Hubbard (born 1938) played trumpet and flugelhorn with various fusion groups. Then, in 1977, he formed the 'hard bop' band V.S.O.P.

ALL-ROUNDER
Chick Corea contributed as a jazz pianist, composer and drummer in Return to Forever, whose albums included Light as a Feather *(1972).*

19

MASTER OF THE FLUGELHORN
Freddie Hubbard excelled on trumpet and its more mellow, bugle-like cousin, the flugelhorn (above). Wayne Shorter joined him in founding V.S.O.P.

CANADIAN TALENT
Oscar Peterson's mastery was in a direct line of descent from legendary jazz pianists Art Tatum (1909–56) and Erroll Garner (1923–77).

ROCK AND FOLK: PRESLEY TO PENTANGLE

Rock now overlapped naturally with folk, country music and blues. This meant that many of the best groups in the Seventies were true one-offs. So was the biggest rock legend of them all, now making a triumphant comeback.

STILL THE KING

The early career of Elvis Presley (1935–77) had seemed a distant memory when, in the late Sixties, he had sensationally rediscovered his form. This now continued with records such as 'The Wonder of You' (1970) and 'Burning Love' (1972) and the films *Elvis – That's The Way It Is* (1970) and *Elvis on Tour* (1973). Despite rapidly declining health, Presley's performing talent never left him.

Elvis carried on singing to the end of his life.

MEGASTAR BAND

Despite (or perhaps because of) a sequence of major changes in their line-up and their move from London to California, Fleetwood Mac became one of the ultimate rock groups of the Seventies, fronted by their two female vocalists, Christine McVie and Stevie Nicks. *Rumours* (1977) was for many years the biggest-selling album of all time (25 million copies). *Tusk* (1979) was another epic success.

FLEETWOOD MAC
After several line-up changes, the band barely resembled its first incarnation as a 1960s blues band.

CSNY
From left,
Nash, Crosby,
Young and Stills.
Despite a
sequence of
fierce personality
clashes, the
quartet produced
some brilliant
music.

CSNY
From left,
Nash, Crosby,
Young and Stills.
Despite a
sequence of
fierce personality
clashes, the
quartet produced
some brilliant
music.

THE EAGLES
Hotel California
overshadowed other
successes by the Los
Angeles-based band,
including On the Border
(1974), One of These Nights
(1975) and The Long Run
(1979), featuring the hit
single 'Heartache Tonight'.

FLYING HIGH

Formed in 1971, the Eagles hit huge
success with their style of country-
influenced rock, which became harder-
edged as the Seventies progressed. Their
albums *Desperado* (1973) and, in
particular, *Hotel California* (1976) sold
millions. The on-off grouping of David
Crosby, Stephen Stills and Graham
Nash was now joined, also on and
off, by Neil Young (born 1945)
(see p. 24). In *Déjà Vu* (1970),
Four Way Street (1971) and *So
Far* (1974), Young brought a
heavier edge of rock to the gentler,
country-influenced sound of the trio.

FOLK IN ENGLAND

The relatively gentle style of Pentangle centred
round vocalist Jacqui McShee and two acoustic guitarists, Bert
Jansch and John Renbourn. They recorded *Cruel Sister* (1970)
and *Solomon's Seal* (1972). Fairport Convention had a much
heavier, electric-guitar sound, featuring the powerful fiddle-
playing of Dave Swarbrick. After *Full House* (1970) and *Angel
Delight* (1971), former lead vocalist Sandy Denny rejoined the
band for *Rising for the Moon* (1975).

PENTANGLE
*The musical mood of large
parts of Seventies England –
coolly attractive, with an
underlying cutting edge –
was summed up in
Pentangle's stylish and
elegant brand of folk. From
left: Renbourn, Danny
Thompson (bass), McShee,
Terry Cox (drums), Jansch.*

RAGE AND RESISTANCE: PUNK AND REGGAE

England produced a deliberately anti-social musical phenomenon in punk rock. Punk's relentless aggression and rhythmic drive caught the angry and embittered mood of the politically turbulent times. It also challenged the self-indulgent extravagance of much Seventies rock.

SOUND AND FURY

The most notorious punk band were the Sex Pistols. They started out in 1975 in London, and disbanded three years later after a stormy American tour, the virtual departure of lead vocalist Johnny Rotten (born John Lydon, 1956), and the death of their bass guitarist, Sid Vicious (born John Ritchie, 1957). The group had already managed to outrage every shade of conventional opinion, which for them, of course, was the whole point. Other bands such as the Clash and the Stranglers joined the punk rebellion.

ANGRY YOUNG MEN
Sid Vicious (left) and Johnny Rotten did not attempt to charm their audiences.

NICE GUYS (AND GIRL)
Blondie's brisk and bright sound led to worldwide hit singles including 'Sunday Girl' and 'Heart of Glass' (both 1978).

22

NEW YORK REBELS

Formed in 1974, the Ramones were America's hard-hitting counterpart to the Sex Pistols.

A BAND WITH ATTITUDE

Talking Heads started out in New York in 1975, led by singer-songwriter David Byrne. More a 'new wave' band than English-style punk, their angry-yet-arty songs nonetheless appealed widely to punk-admiring audiences. Their two best-selling albums, *More Songs About Buildings and Food* (1978) and *Fear of Music* (1979), were produced by Brian Eno (see p. 17).

AMERICA JOINS IN

In the Ramones and the Dead Kennedys, America also produced punk groups with the same anger at the world and the music around them. The friendlier sound of Blondie, fronted by lead vocalist Debbie Harry, indicated that they were really more pop than punk. Part of New York's Seventies 'new wave' of fresh talent and attitude, they were a wild success on both sides of the Atlantic.

23

David Byrne with Chris Frantz (drums) and Tina Weymouth (bass guitar)

CARIBBEAN CHARISMA: BOB MARLEY

With its laid-back but insistently rhythmic sound, reggae developed in Jamaica as a musical symbol of black self-affirmation. Reggae's superstar was Bob Marley (1945–81). During a violent general election campaign in 1978, Marley invited Jamaica's two leading political opponents, Michael Manley and Edward Seaga, to appear on stage with him together, in a gesture of at least outward reconciliation. Neither dared refuse.

BLACK HERO

Bob Marley's superstardom helped to turn reggae into a musical and political symbol of Afro-Caribbean individuality and self-reliance.

THE SONGWRITERS

Songwriting is an individual gift that survives changes in fashion. Several leading figures of the Sixties found they could thrive while adapting their individual styles as they needed. There were talented newcomers, too.

STILL ANGRY AFTER ALL

During the late Sixties, Dylan's brand of folk-rock, with its tough cutting edge, had mellowed into a blander, country-influenced style. Blood on the Tracks (1975) marked the singer's impressive rediscovery of his unique talent.

RARE TALENT

Born Roberta Joan Anderson in Alberta, Canada in 1943, Joni Mitchell was to become an outstanding singer-songwriter. *Ladies of the Canyon* (1970), with its bittersweet, ballad-like songs and lyrics, was a breakthrough success. *Blue* (1971), *Court and Spark* (1974), *The Hissing of Summer Lawns* (1975) and *Hejira* (1976) further developed Mitchell's thoughtful brand of rock and jazz fusion.

Joni Mitchell left Canada to find fame in the US.

TROUBADOURS OF THEIR TIME

Bob Dylan (born 1941) brilliantly rediscovered his best and bitterest form in *Blood on the Tracks* and *Desire* (both 1975). And Neil Young (born 1945) secured his reputation as a master of both heavy (electric) and gentler (acoustic) rock with solo albums including *After the Goldrush* (1970) and *Harvest* (1972). He also appeared with Crosby, Stills and Nash.

24

LOCAL HERO

'Mull of Kintyre', a tribute by Paul and Linda McCartney (left and centre) to their home in western Scotland, featured Wings and the Campbeltown pipe band.

WINGS OVER THE WORLD

When the Beatles broke up in 1970, Paul McCartney (born 1942) released a solo album, *McCartney* (1970), containing one of his best-ever songs, 'Maybe I'm Amazed'. He then toured and recorded with his group Wings, scoring massive successes with *Band on the Run* (1973) and 'Mull of Kintyre' (1977). Elton John (born Reginald Kenneth Dwight, 1947) built a huge following with his brand of piano-accompanied rock. His double album *Goodbye Yellow Brick Road* (1973) included 'Candle in the Wind', which he was later to adapt for Princess Diana's funeral. And a very young Kate Bush (born 1958) shot to instant fame in 1978 with the self-penned 'Wuthering Heights' and the two albums that immediately followed, *The Kick Inside* and *Lionheart* (both 1978).

25

HIGH FLIER

Elton John's Don't Shoot Me I'm Only the Piano Player *(1973) topped the British and American album charts.*

(ANOTHER) FAB FOUR

Abba's Eurovision success with 'Waterloo' was soon followed by the classic singles 'SOS', 'Take a Chance on Me' and 'The Name of the Game'.

TO26738

SWEDEN'S SUPERSTARS

Abba's win in the 1974 Eurovision Song Contest launched the Swedish foursome to world acclaim, spurred on by tracks such as 'Mamma Mia', 'Dancing Queen' and 'Chiquitita'. Benny Andersson's and Bjorn Ulvaeus's songwriting talent – often deceptively simple – was the foundation of Abba's fame.

ENGLAND: BIRTWISTLE TO TIPPETT

England's composers were producing works more individual and sharply contrasted than anywhere else in Europe. And a senior figure found some spectacular late form.

MAXWELL DAVIES MELLOWS (A LITTLE): BIRTWISTLE DOESN'T

ADOPTED ORCADIAN

Peter Maxwell Davies's surroundings in Orkney deeply influenced his music. His opera The Martyrdom of St Magnus (1977) tells the story of the islands' patron saint, and the sounds of the wind and sea inspired Westerlings for chorus (1976).

BIRTWISTLE TOILS

Silbury Hill, a prehistoric English burial mound, gave Birtwistle the title of his Silbury Air (1977) for instrumental ensemble. But much of the Seventies was taken up by work on his vast opera score The Mask of Orpheus (1973–83).

Building on his uncompromising style of the Sixties, Harrison Birtwistle (born 1934) became an increasingly major force with his orchestral work *The Triumph of Time* (1972) and some powerful experiments in music theatre, notably *Bow Down* (1977). Peter Maxwell Davies (born 1934) went to live in Scotland's Orkney Islands, whose landscapes and atmosphere inspired much of his music. *Stone Litany* (1973) was a setting of some local Norse runic inscriptions for mezzo-soprano and orchestra. In 1976, Davies completed his First Symphony.

SPIRITUAL VALUES

John Tavener (born 1944) was exploring musical territory quite different from the post-avant-garde world of Birtwistle and Davies. His style was based instead on the simplicity and power of religious chant, as in his monumental *Ultimos Ritos* (1972). Tavener converted to the Orthodox Church in 1976. His *Liturgy of St John Chrysostom* (1978) was a first major statement of this.

SACRED SOURCE
Tavener's conversion to Orthodox Christianity strengthened his belief that composers should convey religious truths from beyond our understanding, not just express a personal 'inspiration'. But this viewpoint did not prevent him from composing an example of the most non-religious of musical forms: an opera, Thérèse *(1978).*

INTRICATE INVENTION

The music of Brian Ferneyhough (born 1943) explored a style of 'new complexity', notated in extreme rhythmic and expressive detail. Ferneyhough's major work of the Seventies was *Transit* (1977) for amplified voices and instrumental ensemble. This is based on a medieval woodcut of a human figure moving across the boundaries separating Heaven and Earth (the origin of the phrase 'being in one's seventh Heaven').

Ferneyhough is a master of complicated and detailed music.

TIPPETT – APPARENTLY AGELESS

The music of Michael Tippett (1905–98) revealed fresh and remarkable reserves of creative energy. His works became widely popular in Britain and America, helped by a successful recording of his earlier opera *The Midsummer Marriage*. Two new operas now appeared. *The Knot Garden* (1970) was about personality clashes and psychoanalysis. And *The Ice Break* (1977) was Tippett's response to the political and racial troubles of Britain and America in the Seventies.

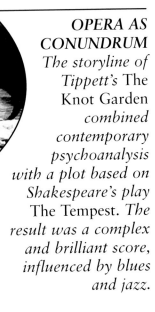

OPERA AS CONUNDRUM
The storyline of Tippett's The Knot Garden combined contemporary psychoanalysis with a plot based on Shakespeare's play The Tempest. The result was a complex and brilliant score, influenced by blues and jazz.

THE END OF AN ERA

For many years, two of the great masters of 20th-century classical music had shown how little 'style wars' mattered when the quality of their work had such depth. Their deaths in the mid-Seventies deprived music of two of its greatest talents.

A HAUNTED SUNSET

The last years of Benjamin Britten (1913–76) were clouded by illness, but creatively he was still at the very height of his powers. He composed an opera for television, *Owen Wingrave* (1971), and another, *Death in Venice* (1973), for the Aldeburgh Festival which he had directed for many years. Britten's last major works – two of the finest he ever wrote – were the cantata *Phaedra* (1975), and a Third String Quartet (1975).

MUSICAL PARTNERSHIP
Britten (left) would have been a different composer without Peter Pears, for whose tenor voice he designed many of his vocal works. And his choice of texts owed much to Pears's knowledge of English literature.

SHADOW OF DEATH

Despite several heart attacks Dmitri Shostakovich (1906–75), too, continued to compose a sombre sequence of late masterworks. These included the last three of his fifteen string quartets (1970–74) and the last music he completed, a Viola Sonata (1975). Shostakovich's Fifteenth and last Symphony (1971) quotes music by two 19th-century composers: Rossini (mock-humorously) and Wagner (seriously).

FINAL INSPIRATION
Britten was much inspired by the musical qualities of particular artists. His cantata Phaedra *(1975) was composed for the great mezzo-soprano Janet Baker. In this rehearsal for the Aldeburgh Festival première, Steuart Bedford conducts the English Chamber Orchestra. Janet Baker is behind him, singing.*

28

MEMORIAL

A bust of Shostakovich outside his former home in Leningrad (now St Petersburg). He worked there on his 'Leningrad Symphony' in 1941 while the city was besieged by the German army.

В ЭТОМ ДОМЕ
ЖИЛ И РАБОТАЛ
С 1937 ПО 1941 Г.
ВЕЛИКИЙ
СОВЕТСКИЙ
КОМПОЗИТОР
ДМИТРИЙ
ДМИТРИЕВИЧ
ШОСТАКОВИЧ
ЗДЕСЬ ИМ СОЗДАВАЛАСЬ
СЕДЬМАЯ
(ЛЕНИНГРАДСКАЯ)
СИМФОНИЯ

Peter Pears *(seated) in* Death in Venice's *principal role, Gustav von Aschenbach*

LATE MASTERPIECE

Britten was offered the choice of immediate heart surgery or the riskier option of continuing work on *Death in Venice*. In effect he shortened his life by insisting on finishing the opera first. It is a dark and beautiful study of fatal emotional obsession. Its leading role was the last major one that Britten wrote for the English tenor, Peter Pears.

THE COMPOSER SPEAKS – OR DOES HE?

After Shostakovich's death, *Testimony*, a ghost-written book of his supposed memoirs, appeared in translation in the West. It portrayed an artist mentally scarred by his experiences of life under Communism, and very different from the image of the proud 'official composer' that was promoted for years by the Soviet authorities. Today the book is still denounced by many as fabrication. But the passing of time and the end of the Soviet era have allowed more information to come out, and a consensus is now forming that the substance of *Testimony* is essentially accurate.

GLOSSARY

AVANT-GARDE An artistic style more challenging than the conventional ones of the time.

BARITONE A middle- to low-register male voice.

BOP (or Bebop) A type of jazz, involving a complex mix of melody, harmony and rhythm. 'Hard bop' is a tougher-sounding offshoot.

CANTATA An Italian term for a work using voices – literally, 'something sung' (also see Sonata).

CHAMBER MUSIC Music to be performed by a group of solo players.

CONCERTO A work with one or more solo instruments and an orchestra.

COUNTRY (short for Country and Western). A type of folk music that originated among white Americans in the rural south, often featuring banjo and fiddle besides guitar.

FLUGELHORN (from the German word for a 'winged horn'). A brass instrument with the full, rounded sound of a bugle, but with the keyed mechanism of the trumpet. It is a popular instrument in jazz.

LEFT-WING Used to describe socialist or communist political views. 'Right-wing' describes conservative political views.

MODERNISM A musical style that sounds modern compared to what had come before.

QUARTET/STRING QUARTET A work for four instruments; also the group that plays them.

SONATA An Italian term for a work for one or more solo instruments – literally, 'something sounded'.

STUDY An instrumental work designed to explore and develop a particular aspect of performing technique and of composing technique. Usually but not always for piano.

SYMPHONY Traditionally, an orchestral work in four or more movements.

TENOR A middle- to high-register male voice – compared to alto (or mezzo-soprano) and soprano, the lower and higher types of female voice. Also used to describe different sizes of saxophone.

TROUBADOUR A travelling singer-songwriter in medieval France and Italy.

WORLD EVENTS

- *Kent State University shootings by National Guardsmen, Ohio*

- *First US and Soviet space missions to Mars*

- *Last US ground troops withdraw from Vietnam*

- *Military coup against Chilean government*
- *War between Israel and Arab nations*

- *President Nixon resigns over Watergate scandal*

- *Death of Spain's dictator General Franco*

- *Death of China's Chairman Mao Tse-tung*

- *US Senate approves financing of neutron bomb*

- *John Paul II elected Pope*

- *Margaret Thatcher elected British Prime Minister*

TIMELINE

	MUSICAL EVENTS	THE ARTS	FAMOUS MUSICIANS	MUSICAL WORKS
0	• August: Isle of Wight rock festival, UK	• Robert Altman's film M*A*S*H released • Death of E.M. Forster, English writer	• Deaths of Jimi Hendrix and Janis Joplin • The Beatles split up • Birth of Mariah Carey	• Deep Purple in Rock • Simon and Garfunkel's Bridge over Troubled Water
1	• Queen play first concert • Benefit concert for people of Bangladesh	• Pablo Neruda awarded Nobel Prize for Literature	• Deaths of composers Igor Stravinsky and Carl Ruggles	• Joni Mitchell's Blue • Shostakovich's Fifteenth Symphony • John Lennon's Imagine
2	• Cinema release of Elvis on Tour • Mar Y Sol festival, Puerto Rico	• Francis Ford Coppola's film The Godfather released	• Carly Simon records 'You're So Vain' with Mick Jagger	• Harrison Birtwistle's The Triumph of Time • Freddie Hubbard's First Light
3	• Led Zeppelin concert in Tampa, Florida breaks US box office record ($309,000)	• Death of poet W.H. Auden • Roger Moore stars in Live and Let Die	• Death of Pablo Casals, Catalan cellist • Death of conductor Otto Klemperer	• Britten's Death in Venice • Pink Floyd's Dark Side of the Moon • Wings' Band on the Run
4	• 300,000 spectators at California Jam see Deep Purple, Black Sabbath and E.L.P.	• Russian writer Alexander Solzhenitsyn exiled to the West	• Mick Taylor quits the Rolling Stones	• Messiaen's Des Canyons aux Etoiles • Stockhausen's Inori • Elton John's Caribou
5	• Keith Jarrett plays The Köln Concert • Film of the Who's Tommy released	• Milos Forman's film One Flew over the Cuckoo's Nest	• Death of Shostakovich • John Lennon retires • Peter Gabriel quits Genesis	• Britten's Phaedra and Third String Quartet • Queen's 'Bohemian Rhapsody'
6	• Paul McCartney tours the US for the first time in ten years • Punk sweeps the UK	• Sylvester Stallone stars in first Rocky film • Death of French writer André Malraux	• Death of Britten • The Clash is formed	• Henryk Górecki finishes Symphony No. 3 • Led Zeppelin's Presence • Abba's 'Dancing Queen'
7	• Saturday Night Fever film sparks disco craze	• Woody Allen directs and stars in Annie Hall • ABC television series Roots	• Def Leppard is formed • Deaths of Maria Callas, Greek soprano, and Elvis Presley	• Fleetwood Mac's Rumours • Michael Tippett's opera The Ice Break
8	• First performance of Peter Maxwell Davies's First Symphony	• Isaac Bashevis Singer wins Nobel Prize for Literature	• David Coverdale forms Whitesnake • Death of Keith Moon, drummer with the Who	• Elliott Carter's Syringa • Kate Bush's 'Wuthering Heights' • Grease soundtrack
9	• Led Zeppelin record their final album	• William Styron's novel Sophie's Choice published	• Deaths of Charles Mingus, jazz bassist and Roy Harris, American composer	• Philip Glass's Satyagraha • Outlandos d'Amour by the Police

31

INDEX

32